The Totally MAD HOUSE COLORING BOOK

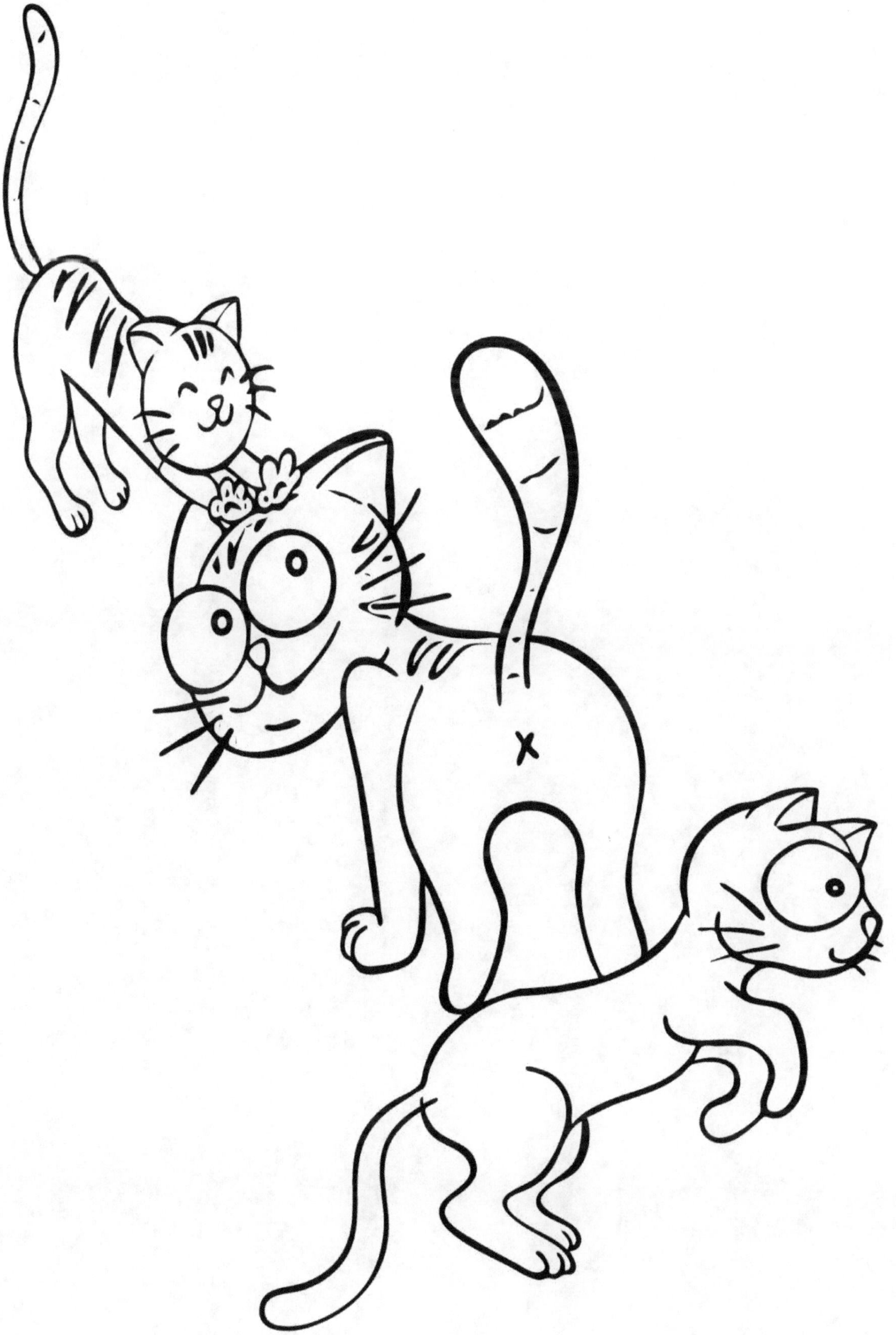

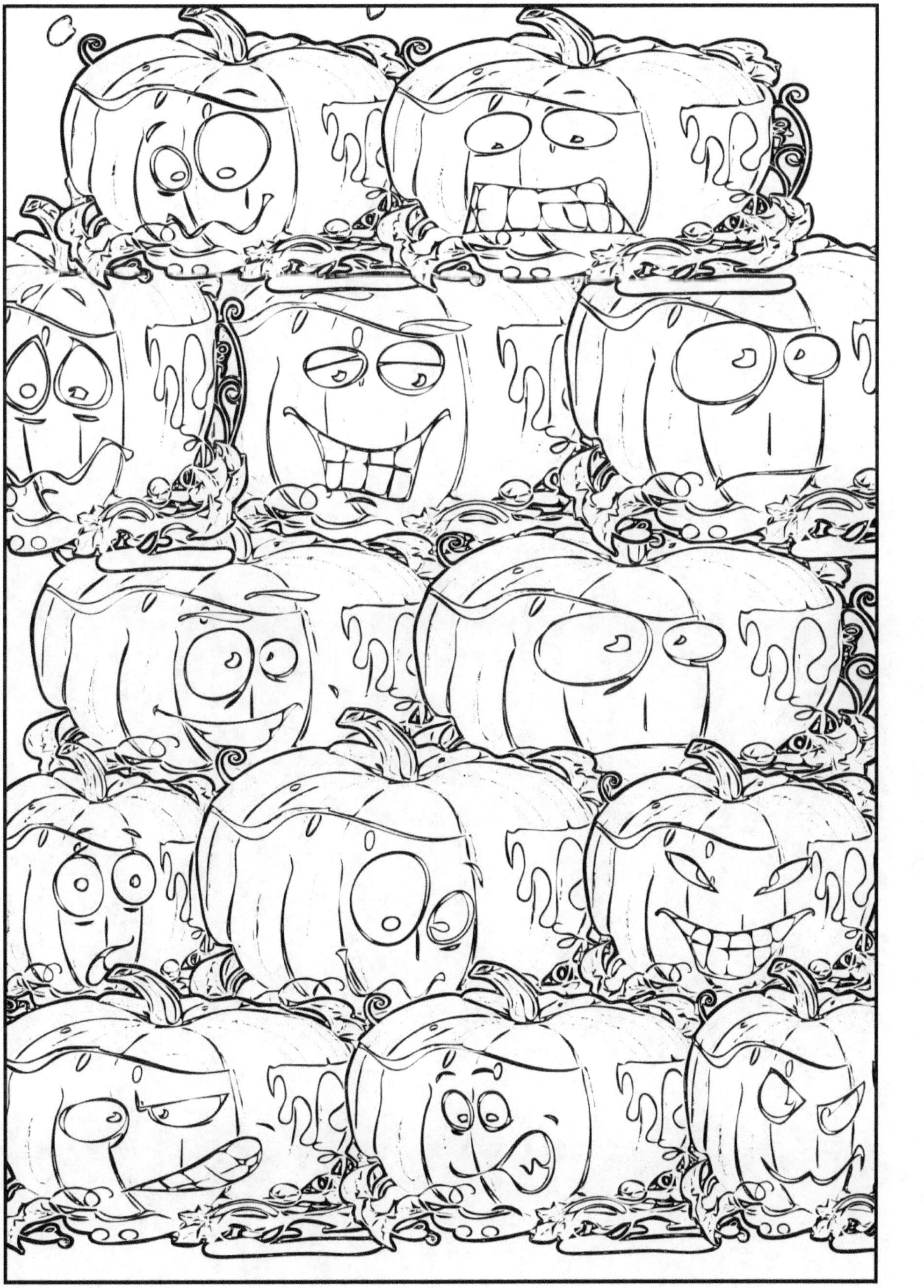

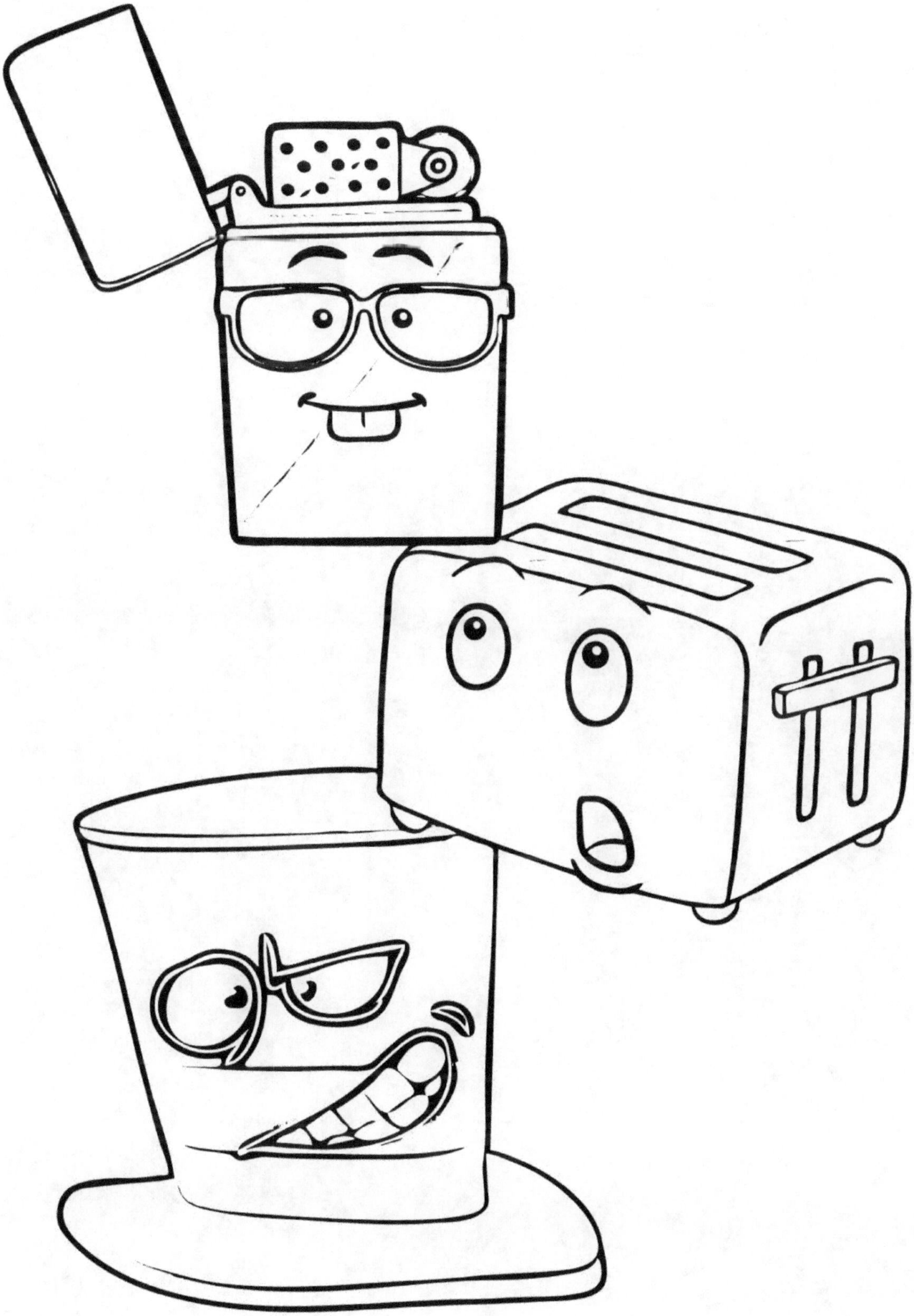

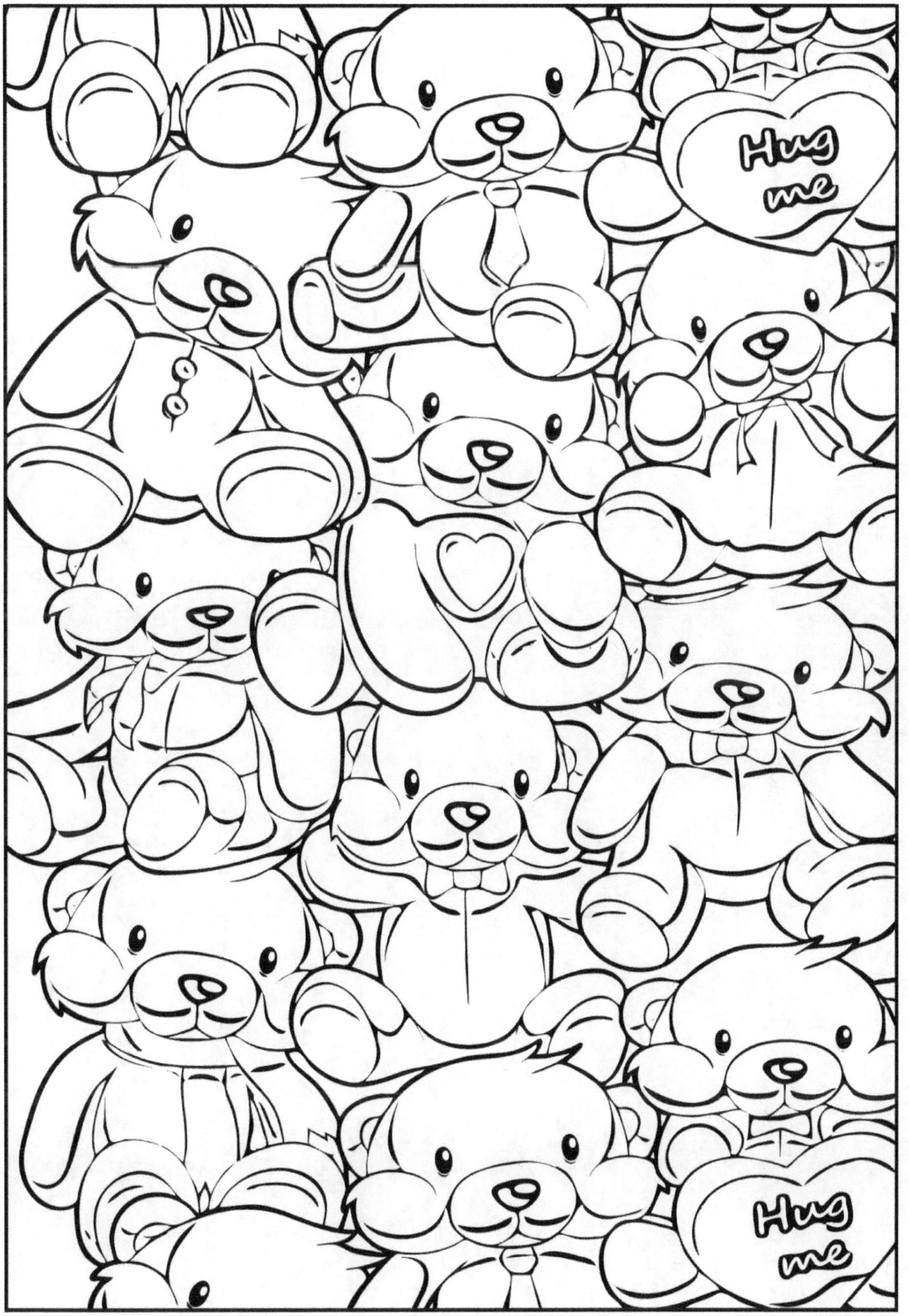
Hug me
Hug me

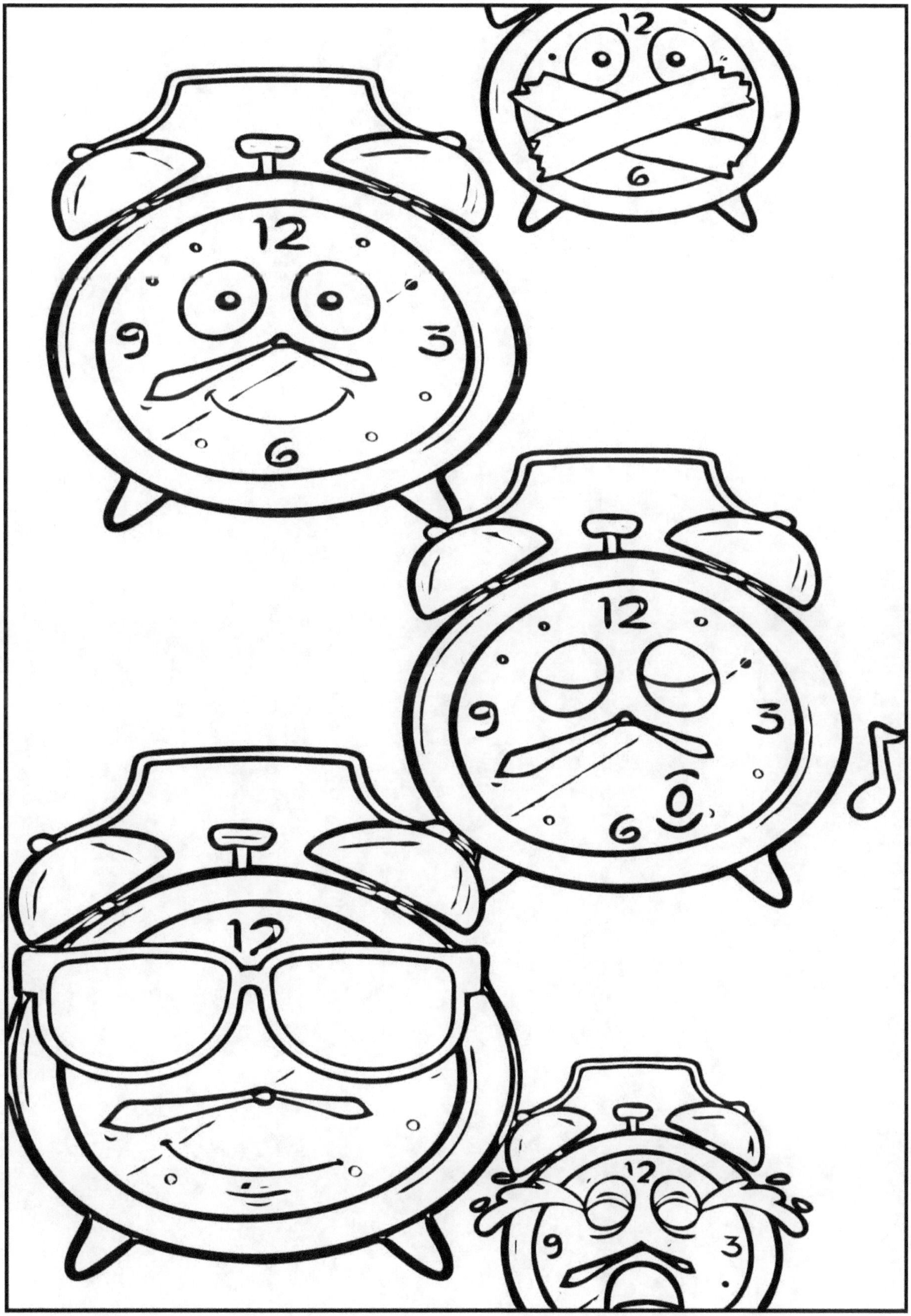

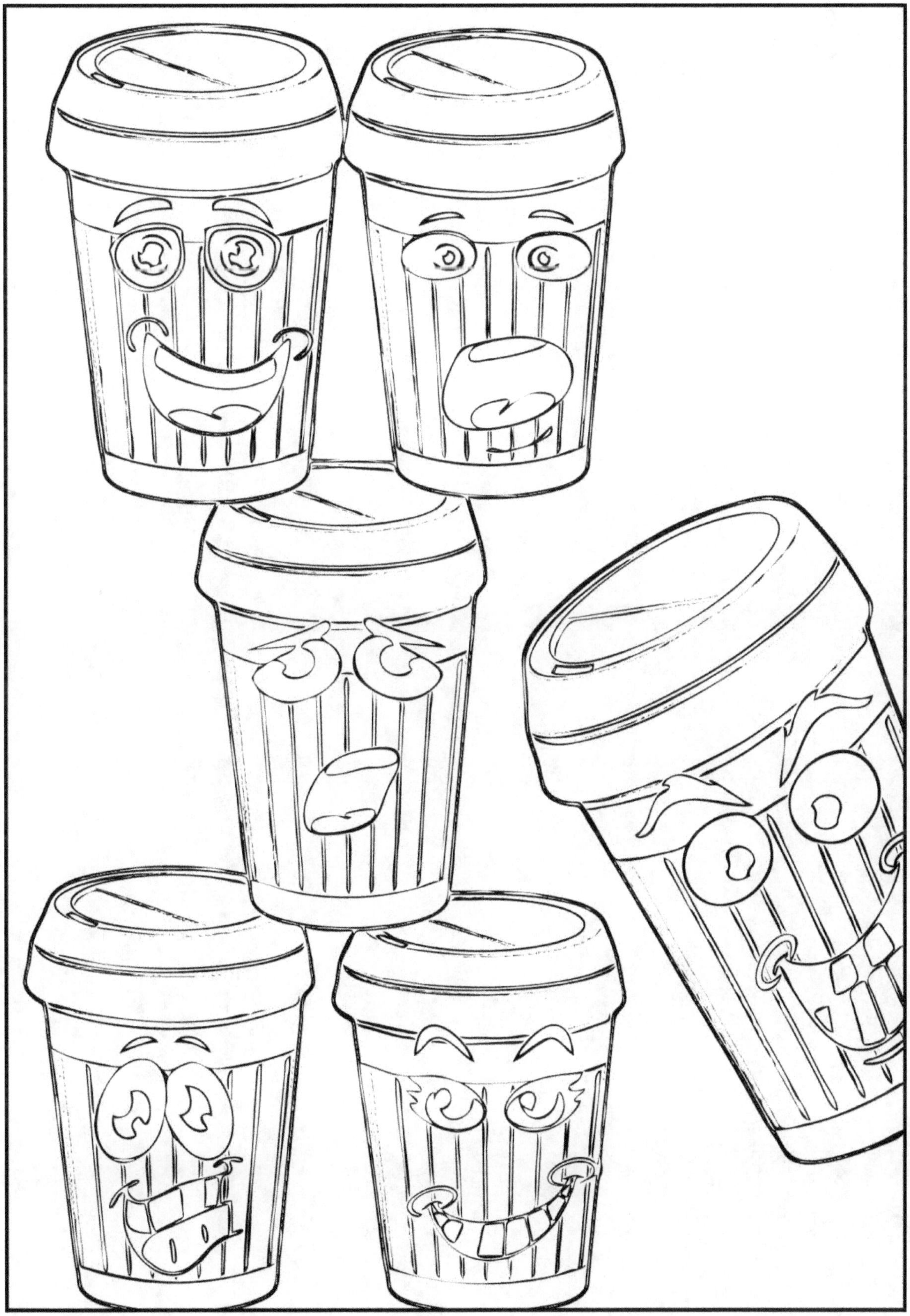

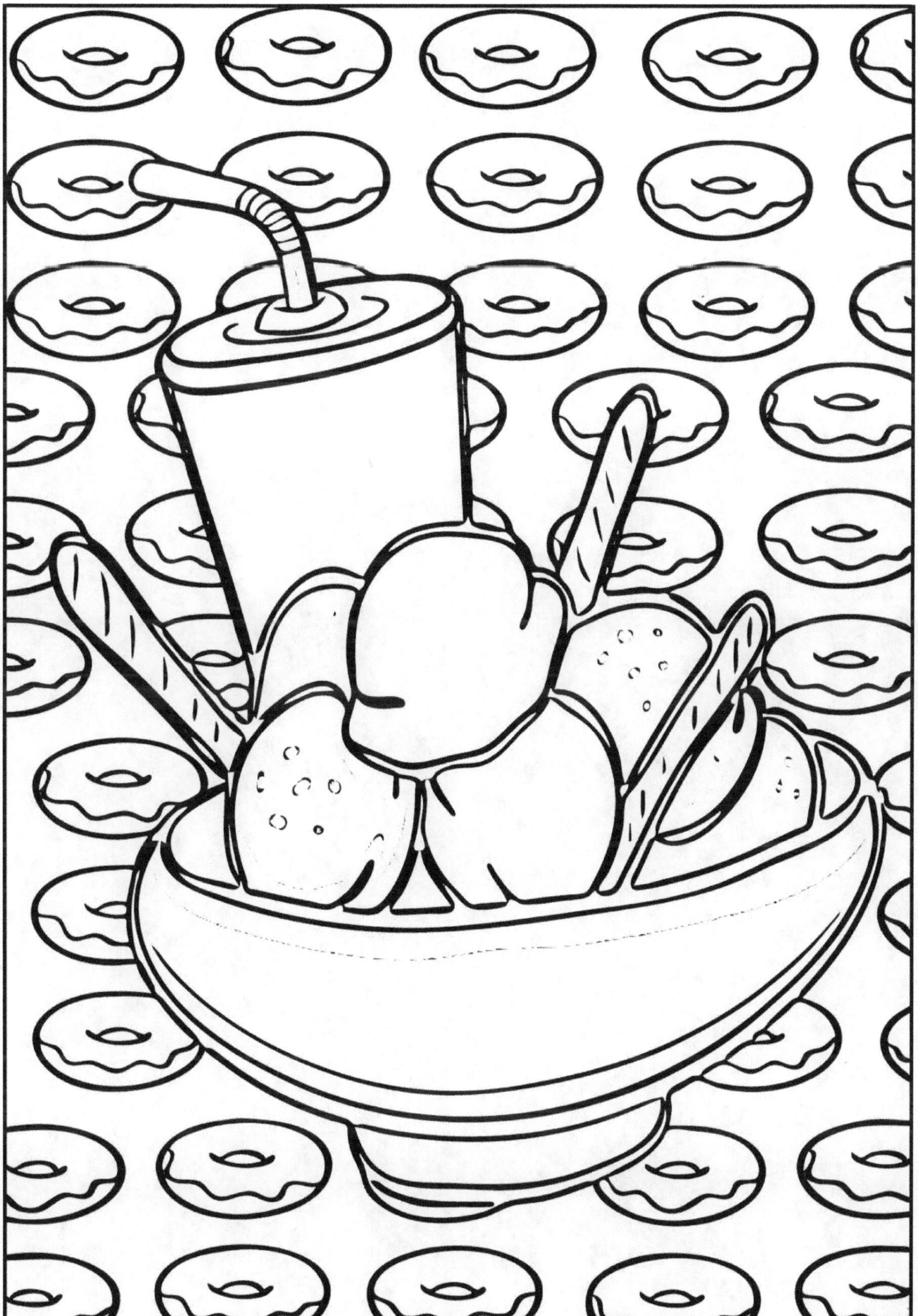

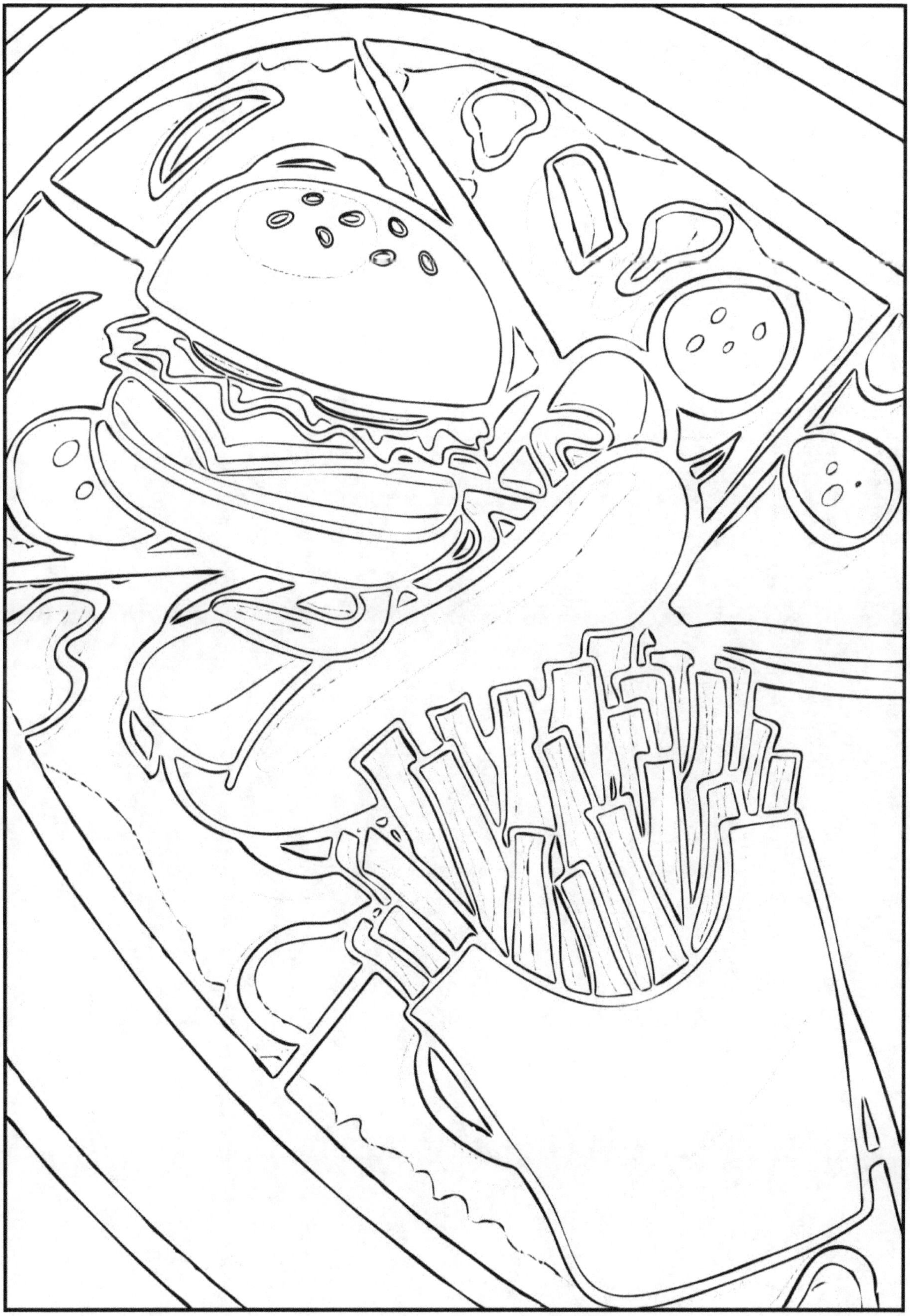

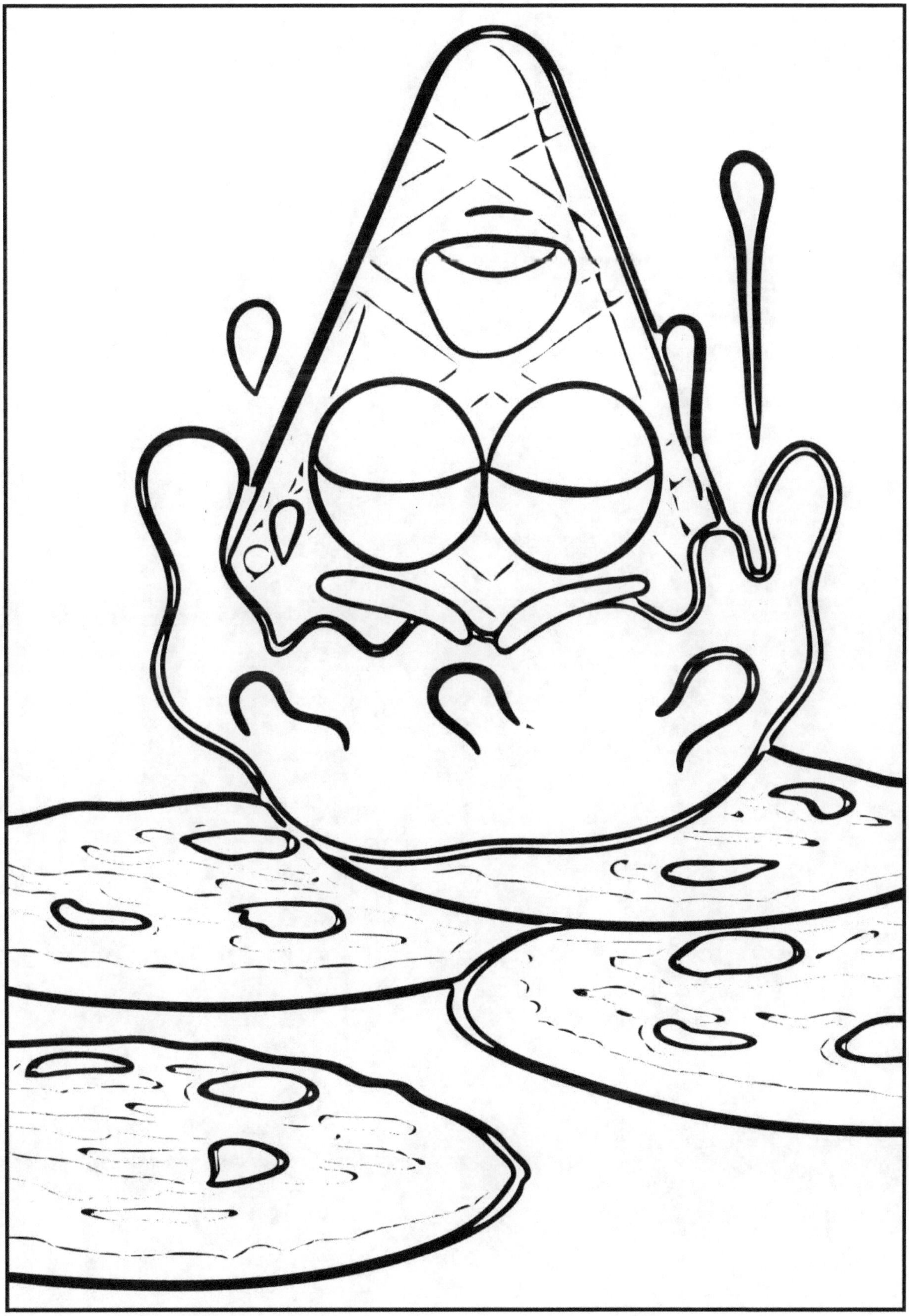

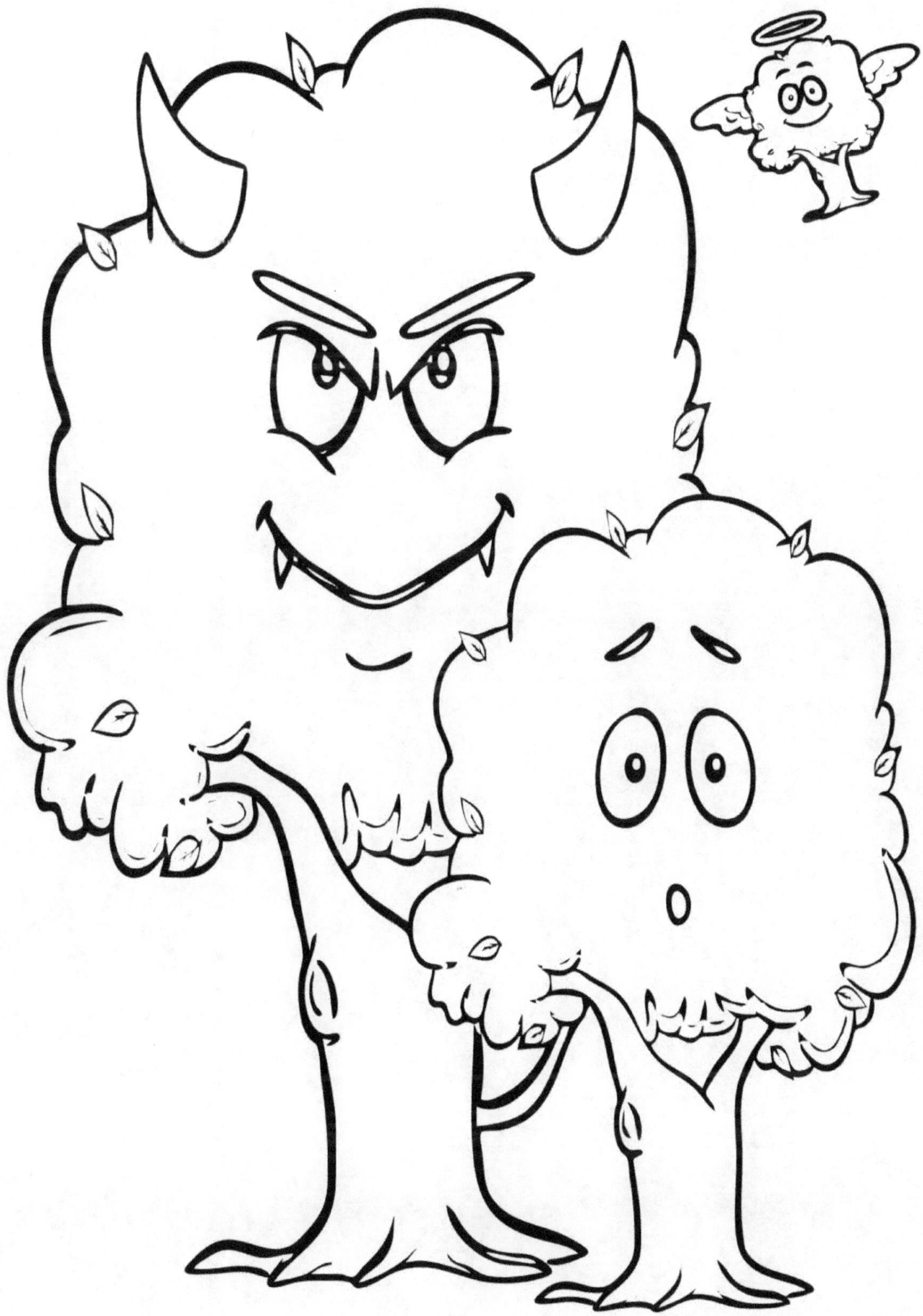

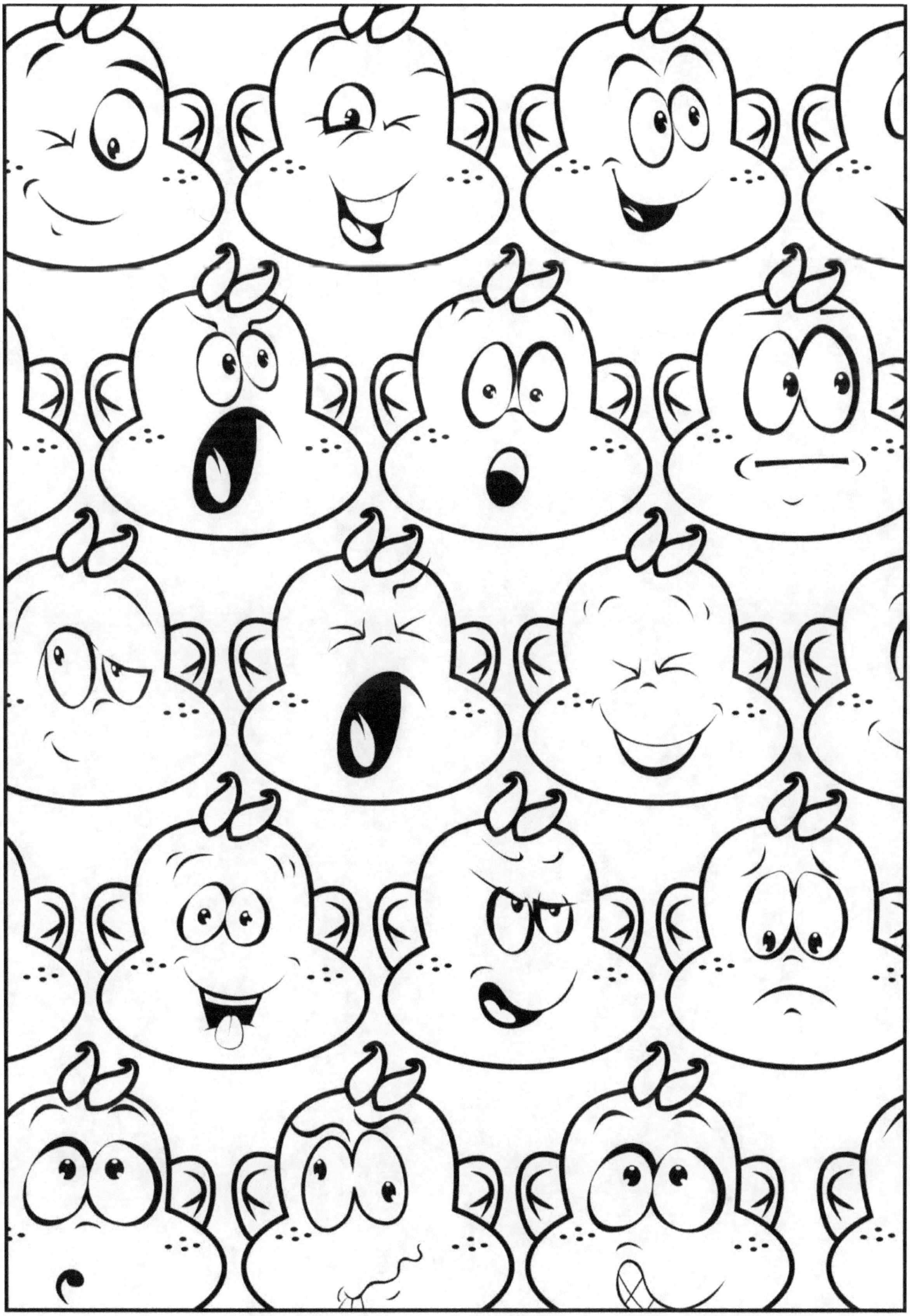

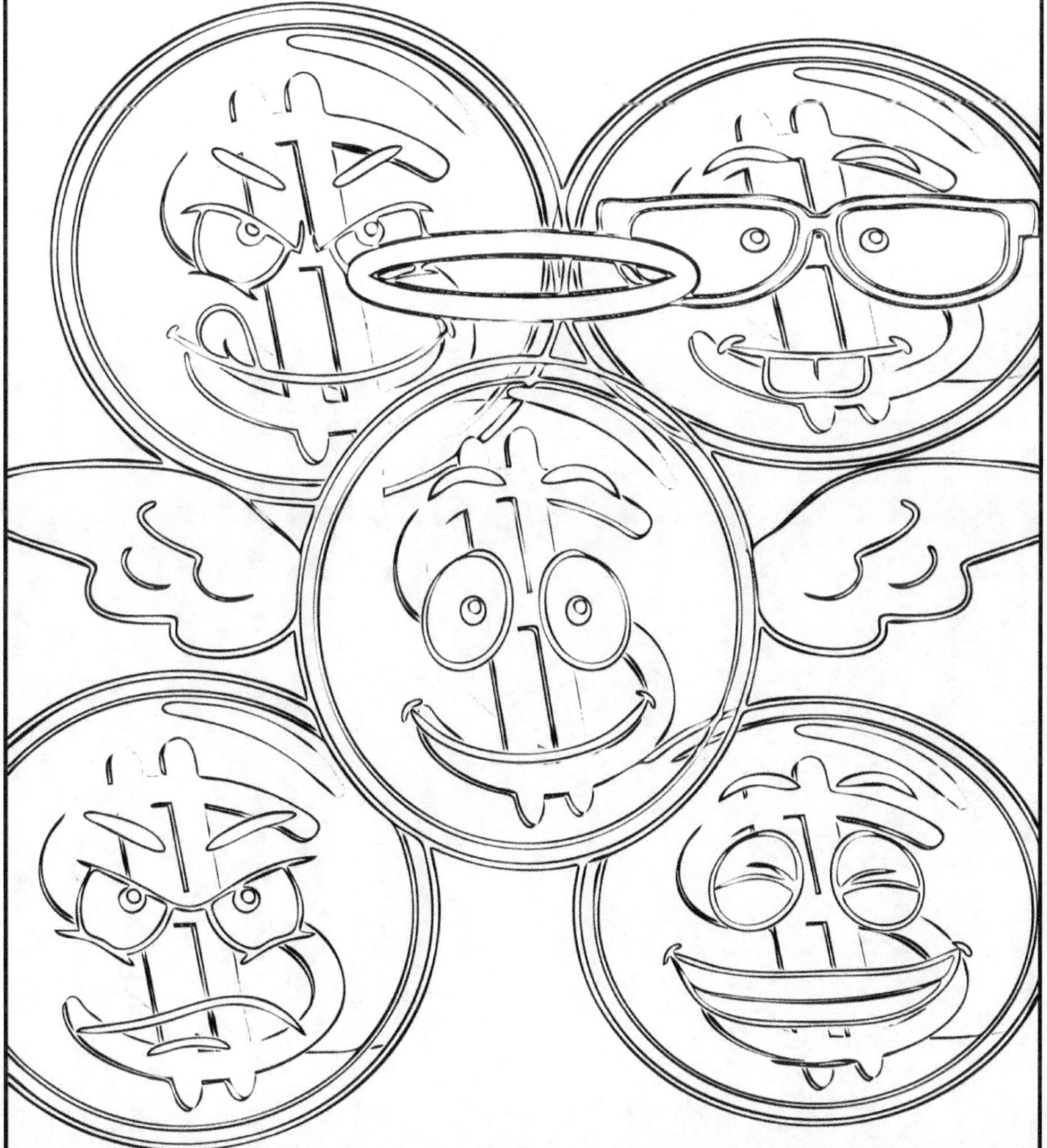

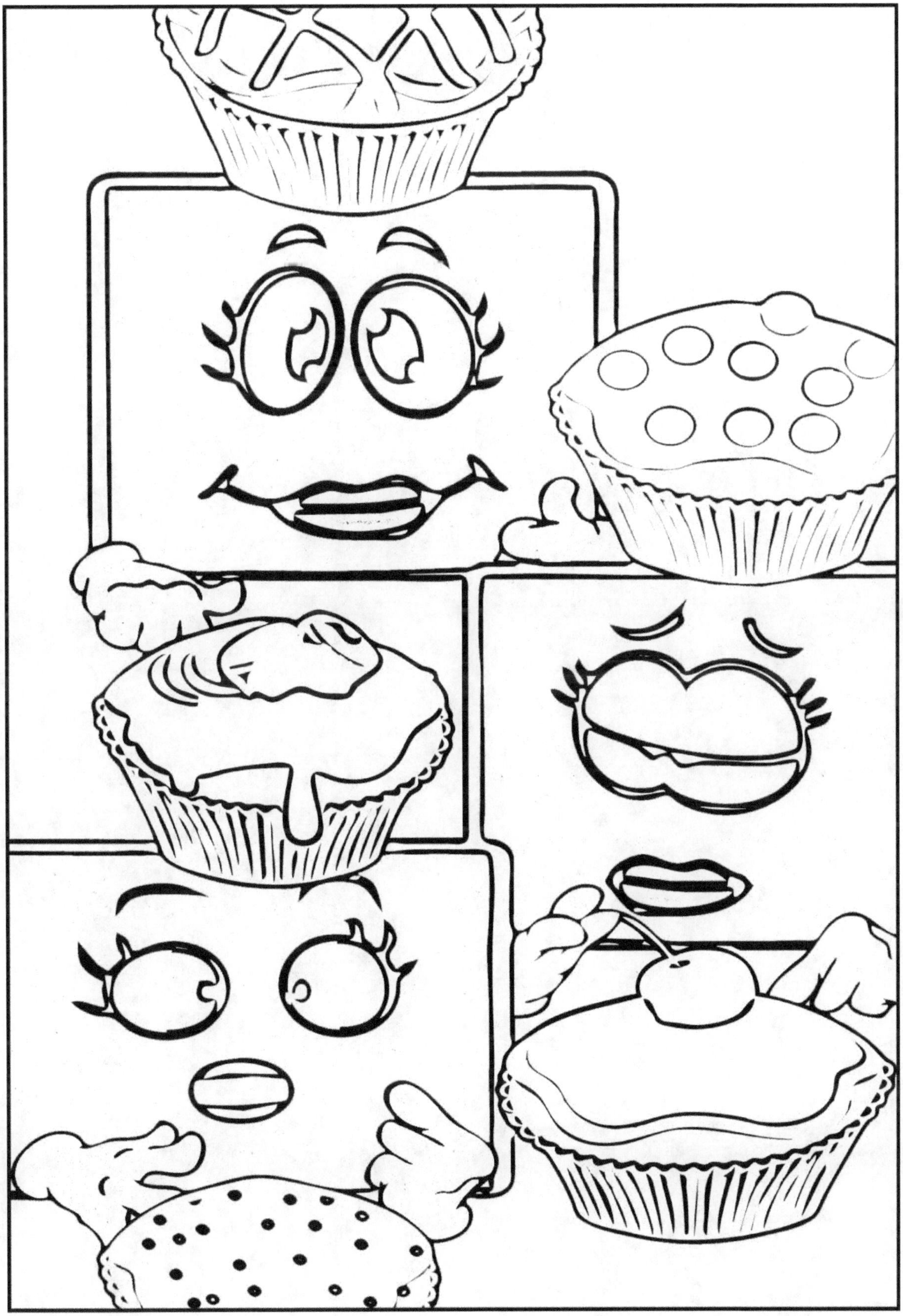

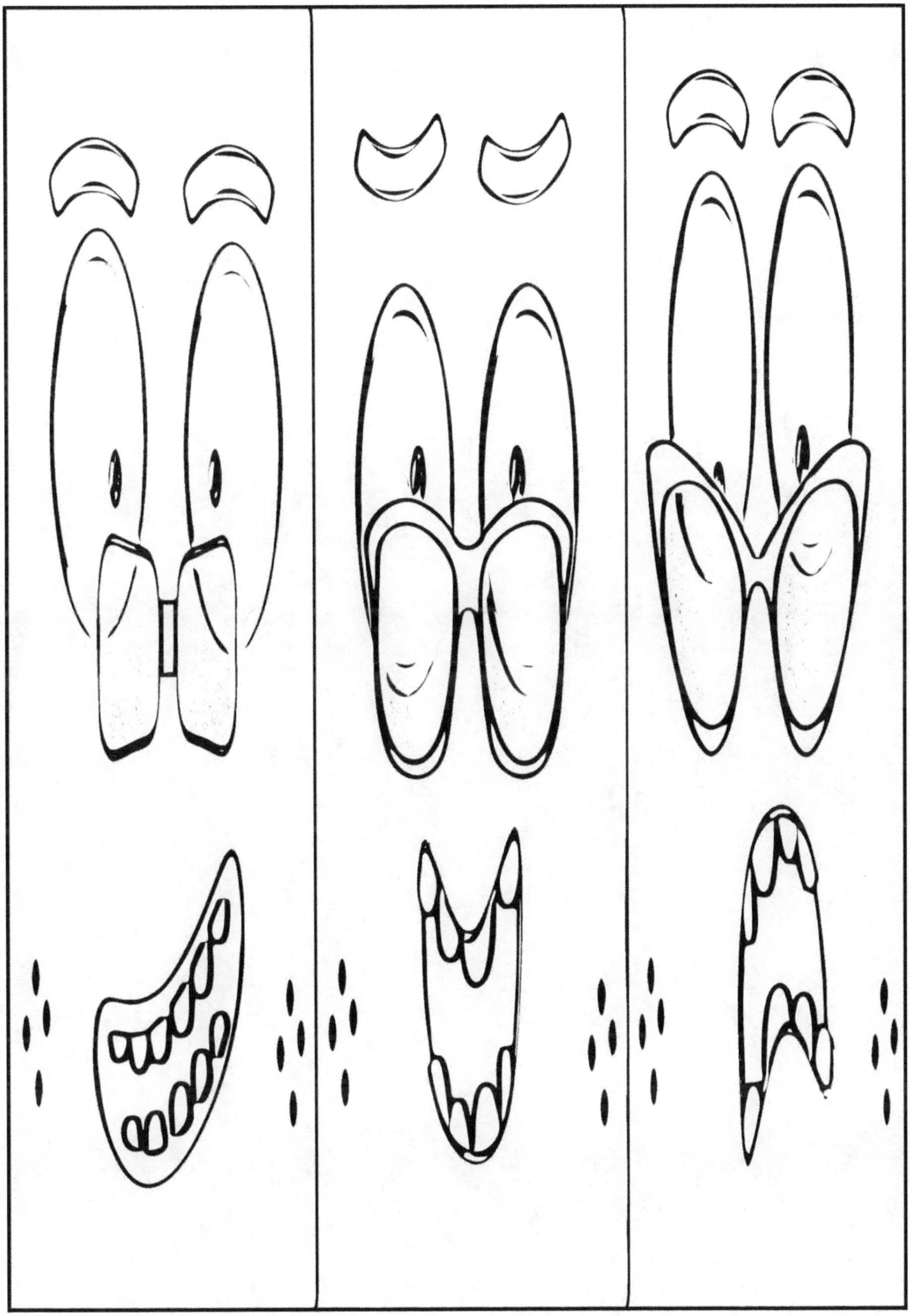

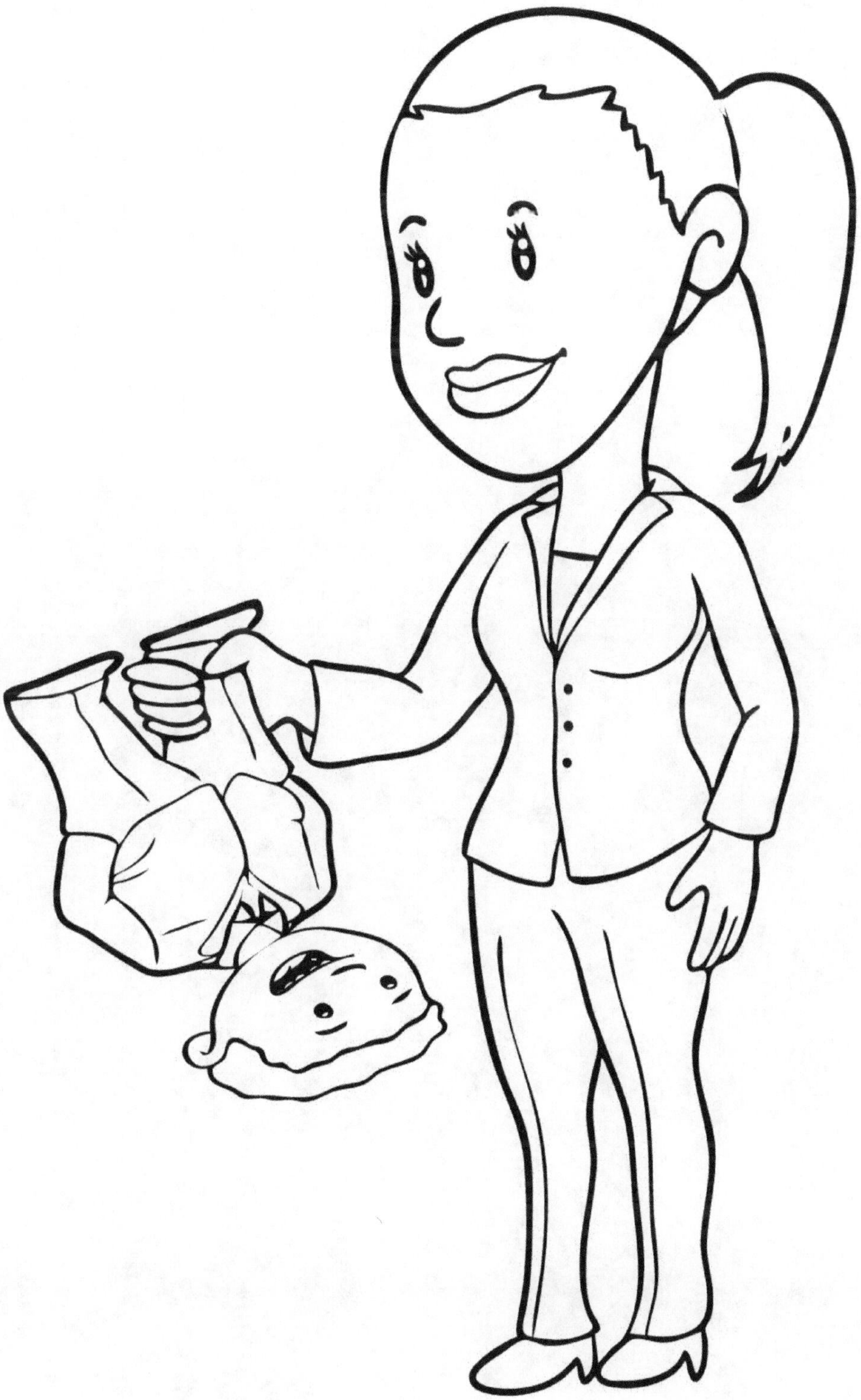

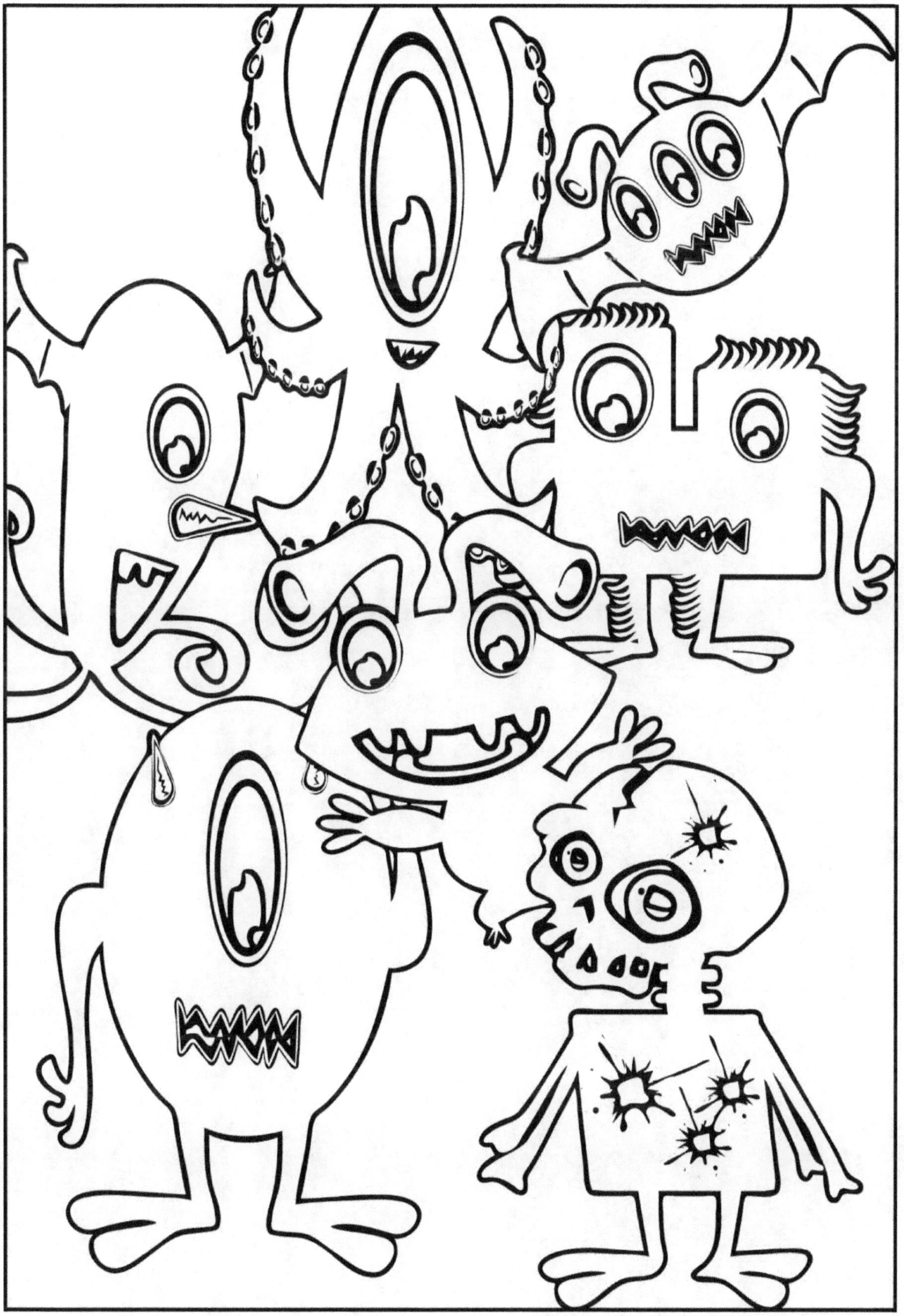

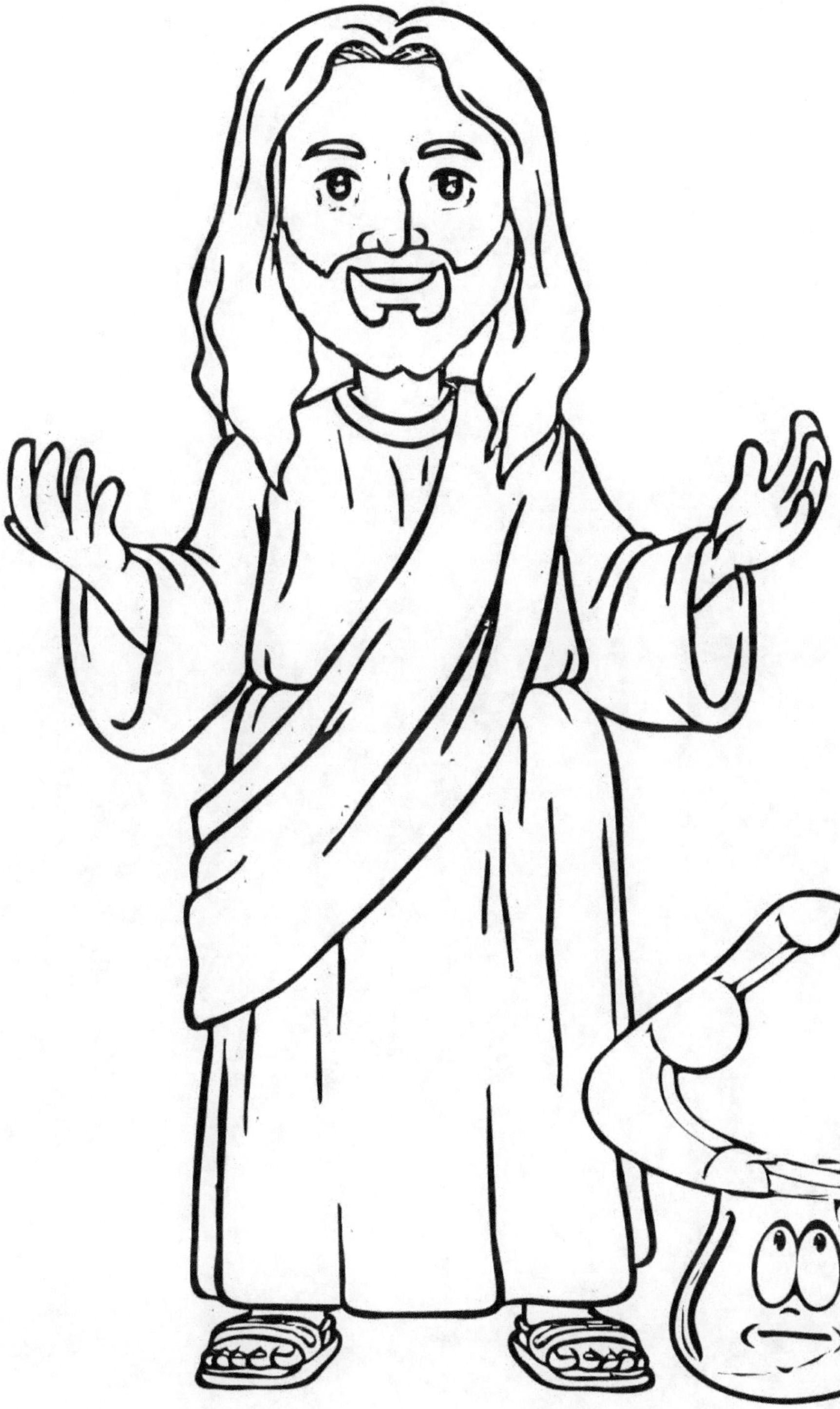

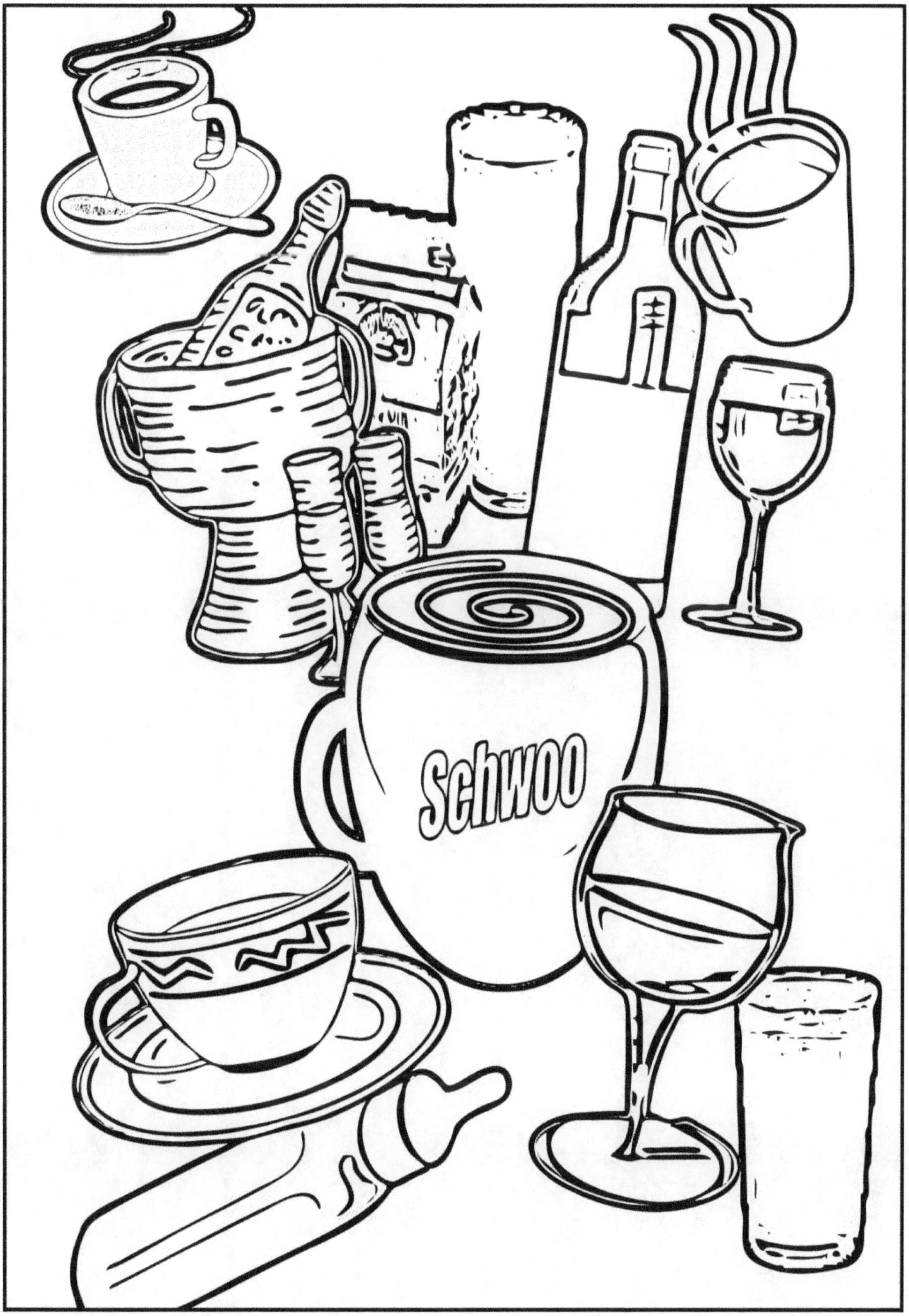
Schwoo

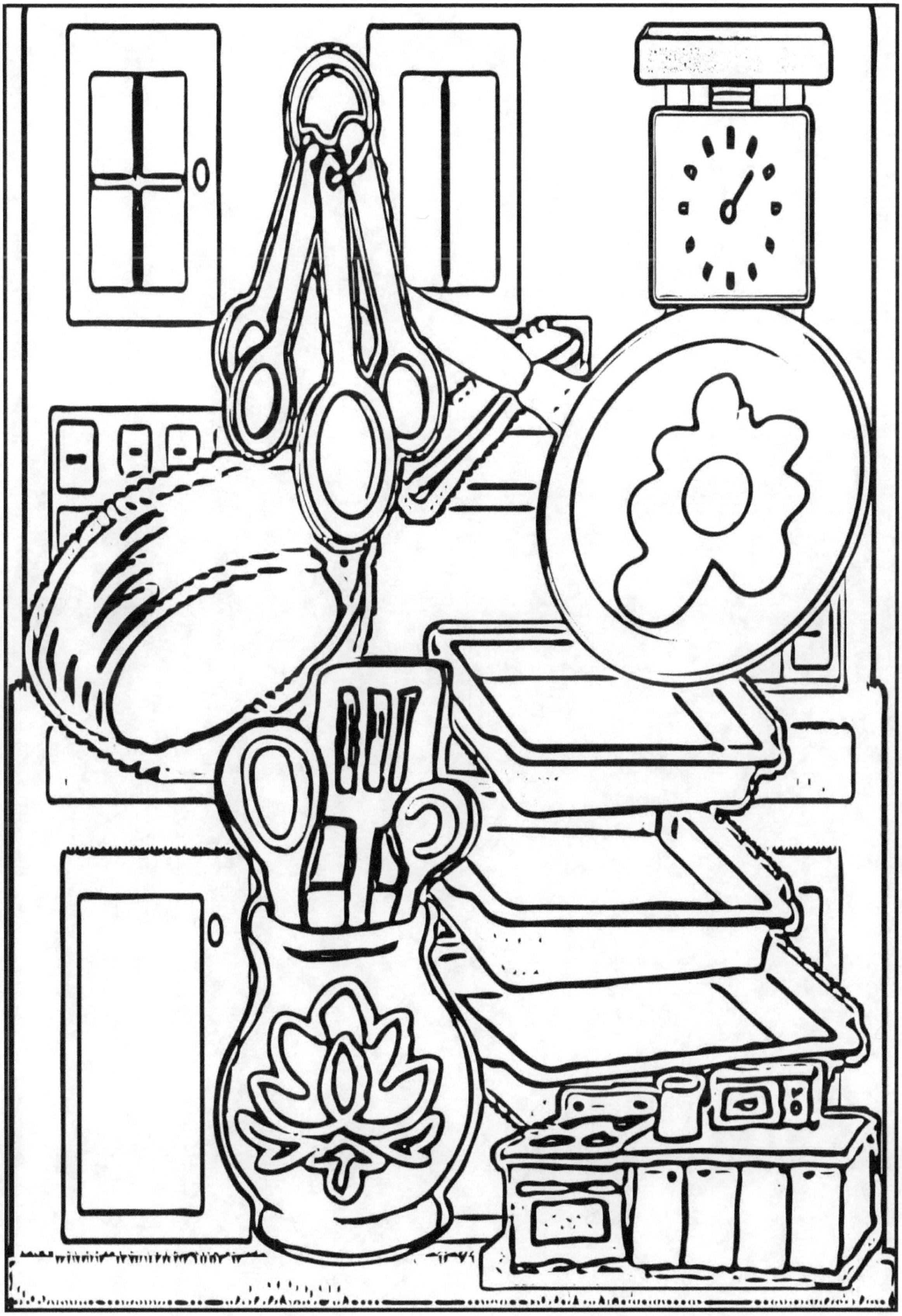

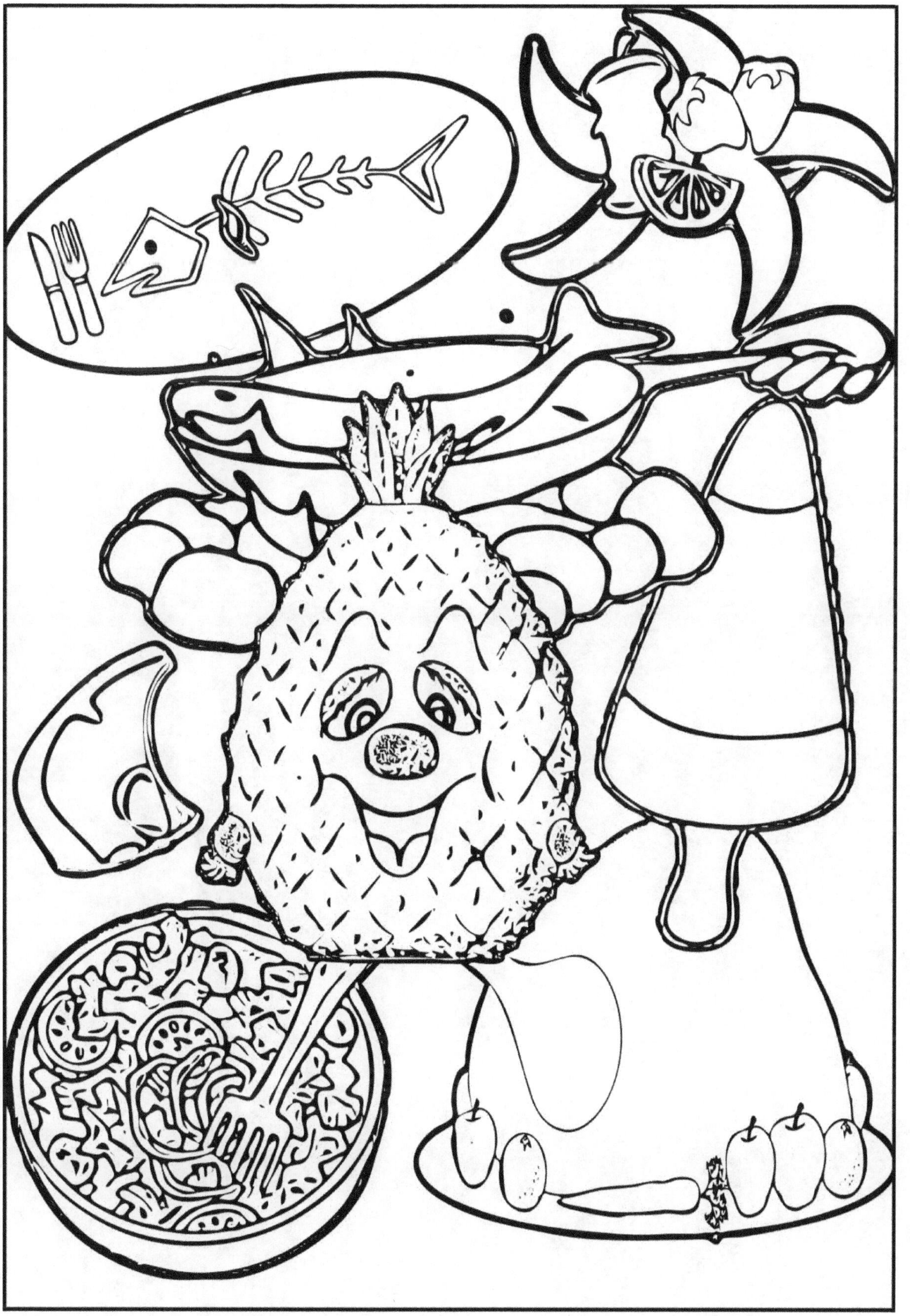

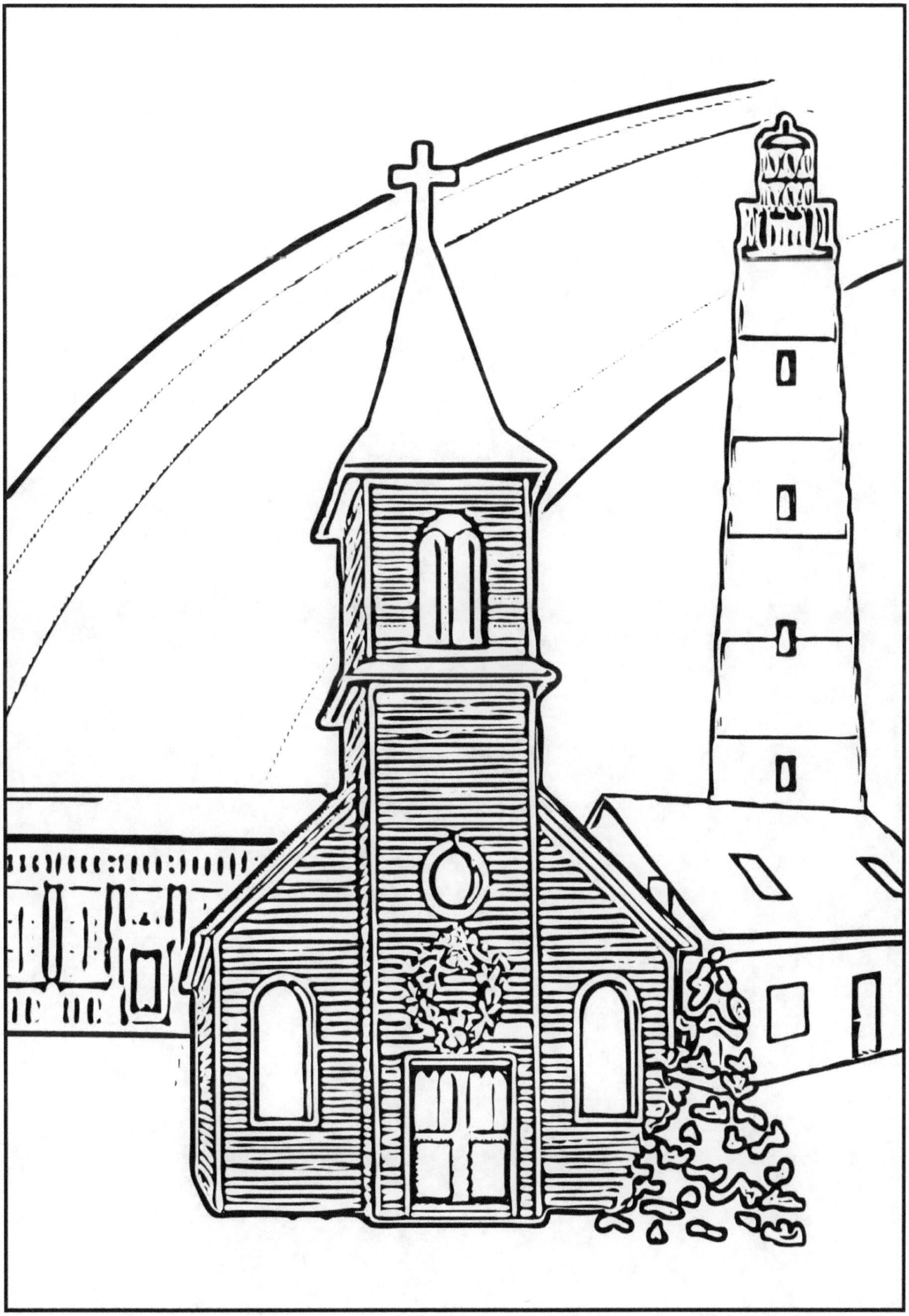

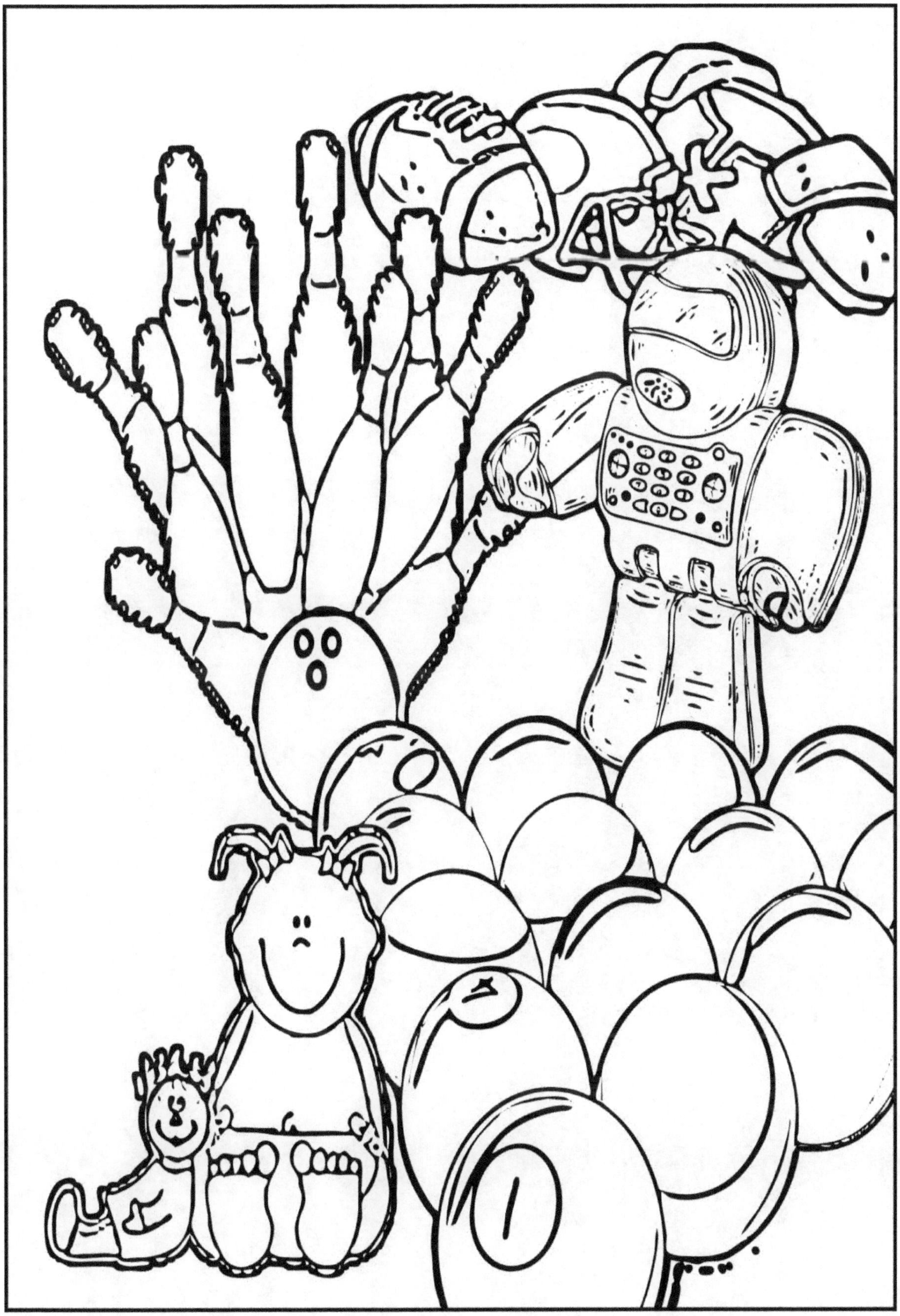

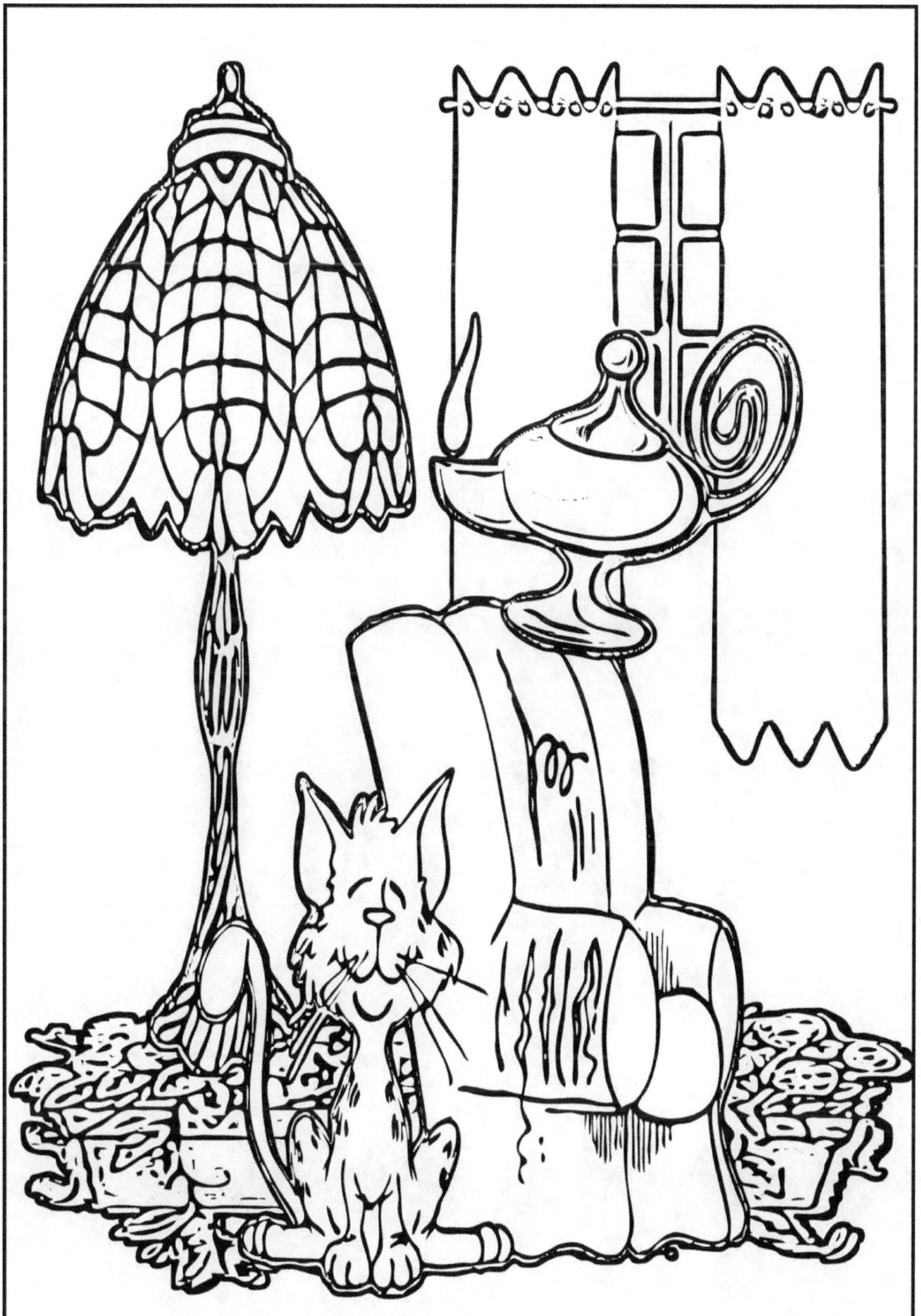

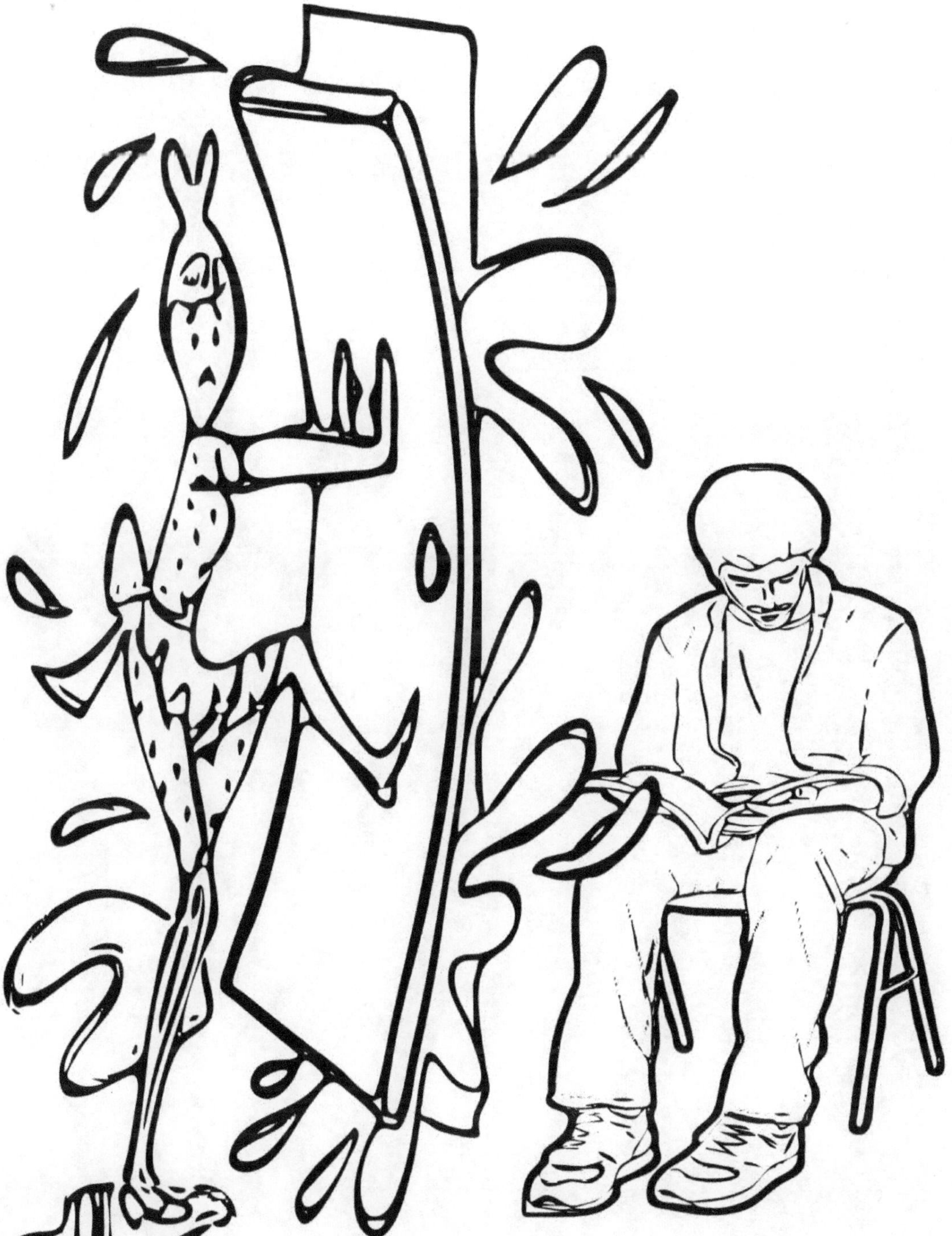

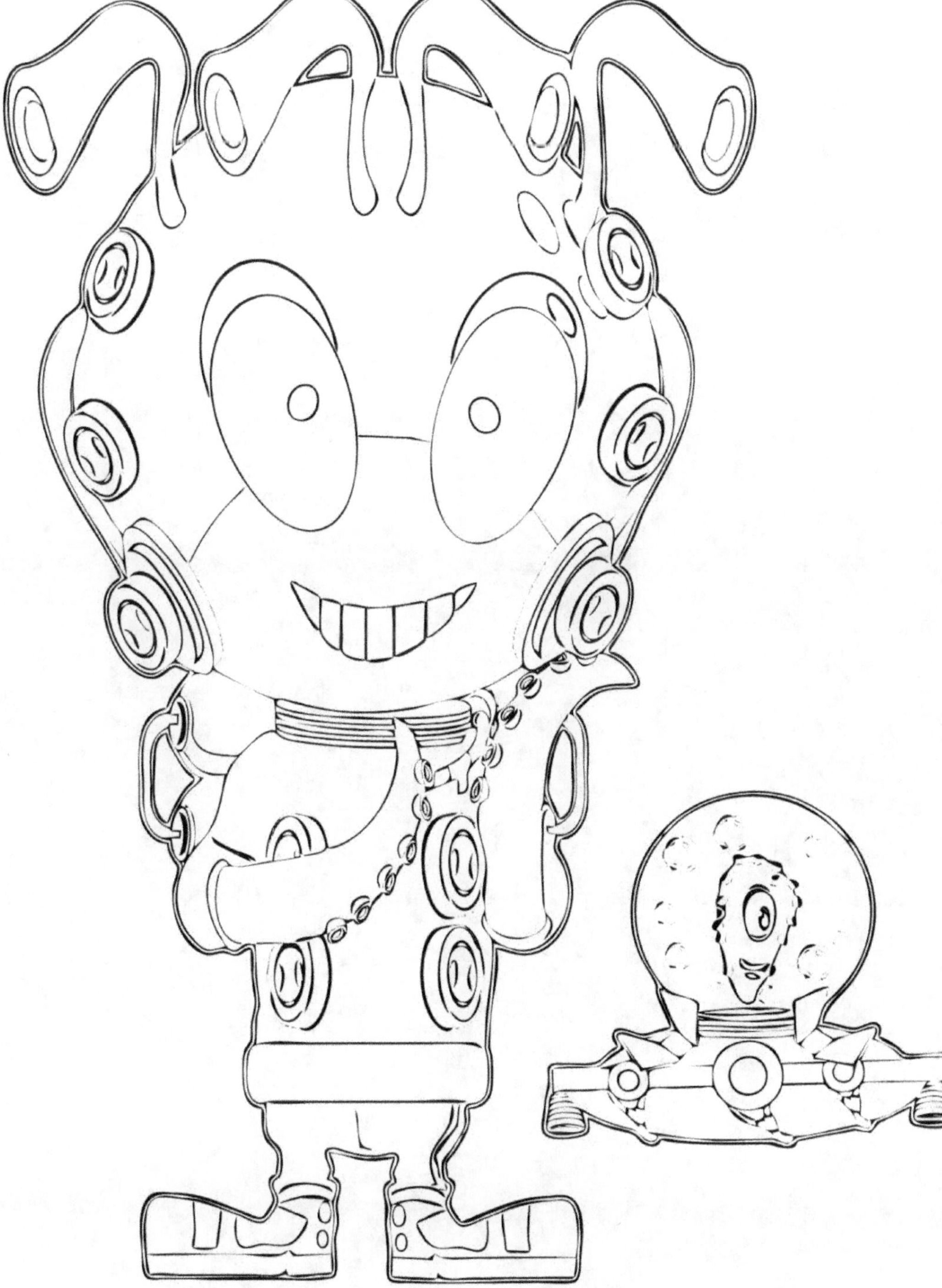

oduct-compliance

2866

5 1 7 6 3 6 0 4 3 *